ALL SAINTS

All Saints Story – Part 1

Boy bands like Boyzone, 3T and Backstreet Boys may well have got used to being on top when it comes to the battle of the sexes, but they'd better hold on to their boxer shorts because girl bands have taken over – and All Saints are the jewel in the crown! With their sultry voices that sound like golden honey laced with warm rum, exciting lyrics and instant sex appeal, these four women (these are definitely women, not girls) are set to explode on the club scene in 1998.

Mix four beautiful girls, fantastic songwriters and vibrant vocalists, stir in a bit of style and add a dash of sexiness and shake with clubloads of rhythm. You've got yourself All Saints, a group of four young women with plenty of talent, ambition and savvy who make music so good it's bad!

All Saints have come into the spotlight slowly... not in a flurry of media sensationalism like some groups we could name, but with carefully selected press coverage orchestrated by their record label, London Records. Thanks to that gradual exposure the four women who make up All Saints – Melanie Blatt, Shaznay T. Lewis and Nicole and Natalie Appleton – are already on their way to becoming big name stars, a process 1998 will surely see completed. And they've done it primarily on the strength of their music – a double dynamite singles salvo, followed by an album so hot you need oven gloves to handle it! But get below the surface and it's quite clear that success for All Saints has been reached via a slow and often tortuous path...

The first formative steps on All Saints' path to success were taken by 13-year-old Shaznay Lewis, who used to spend hours in her bedroom pretending to be a DJ. After introducing each track she would take on the persona of whichever artist she was lining up – whether it be Madonna or Whitney Houston – and tape herself singing. She also used to write down any tunes or lyrics that came into her head: music was clearly a passion she'd had from a very young age. When she was 15 she started entering

Contents

All Saints Story – Part 1	6
Mel's Factfile	10
Mel's Saintly Views	14
Saints in Love	16
All Saints Story – Part 2	20
Nic's Factfile	24
Nic's Saintly Views	28
Fame and Fashion!	30

All Saints Story – Part 3	36
Nat's Factfile	40
Nat's Saintly Views	44
Saints or Sinners?	46
Shaznay's Factfile	52
Shaznay's Saintly Views	56
A–Z of All Saints	58
Acknowledgements	64

First published in 1998 by Virgin Books
an imprint of Virgin Publishing Ltd
332 Ladbroke Grove, London W10 5AH

Copyright © 1998 Virgin Publishing Ltd

Designed by Slatter-Anderson

First published in the United States in 1998 by Billboard Books, an imprint of Watson-Guptill Publications, a division of BPI Communications, Inc., at 1515 Broadway, New York, NY 10036

All rights reserved. No part of this publication may be reproduced, stored in a retrieval system, or transmitted in any form or by any means – electronic, mechanical, photocopying, recording, or otherwise – without prior permission of the publisher.

Library of Congress Cataloging-in-Publication Data for this title can be obtained from the Library of Congress.

ISBN 0 8230 8255 5

Printed and bound in Great Britain by Butler and Tanner Ltd, Frome and London

First printing 1998

1 2 3 4 5 6 7 8 9 / 06 05 04 03 02 01 00 99 98

ALL SAINTS

THE UNOFFICIAL BOOK

All Saints are the jewel in the crown.

competitions which then led to session work doing backing vocals for Ben Volpeliere-Pierrot (the former lead singer of 1980's popsters Curiosity Killed The Cat) and Don-E. Shaznay then met Melanie Blatt while doing session work at a west London recording studio on the All Saints Road. They joined together in 1994 with a third member, naming themselves after the road (and, initially at least, with 1.9.7.5. tacked on to the end). They were briefly signed to ZTT Records, releasing two now forgotten singles. Their first live gig came on *Touch* magazine's stage at the Notting Hill Carnival – but, as Mel explains, the trio didn't know what direction they wanted to go in and the record company didn't either so it was a pretty short-lived thing.

The third member then left the band to go solo, leaving co-songwriters Mel and Shaz looking for a new vocalist. A few months later Mel's dad happened to bump into Nic Appleton who had been really good mates with Mel at school until she'd moved away to New York several years earlier. Nic, Nat and Mel had been at school together for ten years so were thrilled to meet up again – and, fortunately for us, they picked up just where they'd left off. Nic was persuaded to leave her job and join the band as a singer and that was when things really started happening. But success didn't land straight in their laps. When they started the group there were few, groundbreaking all-female bands around, and to make matters worse they were not experienced in dealing with record companies. In the early days they were dogged by dodgy record deals, rip-off merchants and frustration. Mel remembers crying her eyes out in bed at night from pure frustration, waiting for their big break. Would it ever happen for these four wannabes?

Mel

Angelic Melanie sees herself as more of a saint than a sinner

Full name: Melanie R. Blatt

Nickname: Mel-odie… among others. According to Mel, Shaznay calls her Smell and Nic and Nat call her Bucket – so take your pick!

Date of birth: 25 March 1975

Age: 22

Star sign: Aries

Eyes: Brown

Distinguishing marks: Pierced ears and musical notes tattooed on her right arm

Lives: Ladbroke Grove, London, with her parents and 10-year-old sister Jasmine

Likes: Cooking and cookery programmes on TV

Dislikes: People who whinge

Ambition: For All Saints to be as great as her music idols Missy 'Misdemeanour' Elliot and Blackstreet

Life before All Saints: She once worked in swank designer clothes shop Kookai but only lasted from 10am until 1pm when she walked out! Otherwise, there have been small parts in TV adverts

Music that gets her buzzin': Mel has got bags of respect for Stevie Wonder because he's influenced all her favourite artists. She listens to garage, R&B and hip-hop

Earliest memory: Mel remembers vividly her excitement when her little sister was born when she was about 11 or 12. She gets on with her sis really well and loves her to bits

Which Saint is she? Melanie reckons she's the organizer of the group. She carries around everything from aspirins to chewing gum in her bag in case somebody needs it. She describes herself as calm, jokey and generous. She reckons she's nice, but can't speak for the rest of the group's feelings

Saint or sinner? Angelic Melanie sees herself as more of a saint than a sinner but admits she keeps a foot firmly in both camps depending on her mood

Perfect man: She confesses to liking boxer Robin Reid… especially when he's dripping with sweat

What the other Saints say: She's the nurse of the group

Fave hunk: Jay from Jamiroquai

Closely guarded secret: Melanie was in a toothpaste advert with Baby Spice

Mel

Tough and confident on the outside but a jelly on the inside, Melanie has had a rough ride to achieving her aim of being in a band and producing good music. Mel first met pal Nic at the Sylvia Young Theatre School she attended with Emma from the Spice Girls. According to Mel they weren't best mates or anything but they'd say hello. Mel hung out with pal Nic and Denise van Outen (of *Big Breakfast* fame) but reckons none of them was ever put forward for auditions because the school had its favourites! She freely admits she's a cynic!

She then moved to France because she needed an operation on her back. Her mum was fed up with being told that Melanie might end up paralysed, so she upped sticks and took her to a small village full of elderly *messieurs*. Without a word of French, Mel found changing from an English to a French school the most difficult challenge of her life to date. Still, Mel's a fighter: she settled down quickly and, after a successful operation (she now has a big scar on her back which is held together by metal pins), she returned to England, speaking fluent French and with heaps of ambition.

Melanie has always enjoyed cooking and was thrilled when Nic took her to see her favourite programme *Ready, Steady, Cook!* being filmed. Mind you, Shaznay isn't as enthusiastic about Mel's cooking: the last time she ate Mel's food she was sick for days after! Nic and Mel are bosom buddies and have a really good laugh together. Nic says Mel is the nurse of the group and always has tablets in her bag. Mel says Nic is mad! Though Mel is absolutely gorgeous, with bags of talent, she says she suffers from low self-esteem and self-confidence, particularly in her private life. She hasn't had a lot of luck in love. She admits she is not a very good flirt even though Nic has tried to give her lessons. We reckon she'll be beating the guys off with a stick before long! She's very close to her family and says her parents are hippies – in fact, one of her earliest and happiest memories is of going to the Glastonbury Festival when she was 6 and playing her violin on top of her parents' car! Weird…

She doesn't think of herself as a girls' girl and finds boys are generally a lot more honest. Her best girl pals are in the band. She always talks to her friend Martin, one of her two best friends (both boys), if she's upset.

Mel likes to be in control and used to be heavily involved with the business side of the band. Now she's too busy for that but she finds it difficult not to be so involved. It freaks her out if she thinks something's going down that she doesn't know about! Nowadays she prefers to keep the private side of her life to herself and still finds all the attention difficult to take. She finds it hard to show her feelings to people on any subject: if the press prints something confidential about her she'll be embarrassed but will shrug it off as if she doesn't care… even if deep down she does.

Mel doesn't think she sticks up for herself as much as she should because nine times out of ten she can't be bothered to argue. Being in All Saints has really built her confidence and she's proud of what they've achieved together. She's glad they all feel that their music takes priority and that the rest of the girls keep her sane.

Mel's Saintly Views

On the Spice Girls
Mel thinks the Spice Girls are cool and that it's amazing how they've become such a massive phenomenon. She reckons All Saints are much better looking and have got more upstairs!

On decorating
She's not into flowers and frills. She's a beige decor person… and that's it!

On getting drunk
The cheapest thing to get Mel drunk on is white wine and blackcurrant liqueur. After three of those, she's giggling and singing… but she doesn't drink a lot these days because she's too scared of throwing up.

On her favourite animal
Mel would like to be a tortoise because they laze around all day.

On her least favourite animal
Mel hates her sister's dog. She says it's white, fluffy and licky and wees all over the place.

On knickers
She owns hundreds of pairs of pants which she buys in France or Marks & Spencer.

On babies
If she had children she'd call them Lip and Sot!

On cooking
She can cook anything, from cheese fondue to lamb meatballs. She loves cooking and she is the chef of the band: maybe that's her French side coming out!

On a good night out
When she's not working on a Saturday night she enjoys going to the Complex (trendy London club) or Browns (swanky showbiz joint) and having a whizzo time with her mates.

On her little sister
Mel shares a bedroom with her sister Jasmine and half the bedroom is covered in Barbies and Hanson posters. She admits they argue sometimes, but really they love each other.

On her favourite films
Mel loves *Gone With The Wind* because it's a classic and she adores Clark Gable.

She's not into flowers and frills. She's a beige decor person… and that's it!

Saints in Love

All Saints may sing about sex, love and guys – but what is it about a bloke that turns them on. And what type of man wouldn't they be seen dead with? Read on, and all will be revealed!

Men They Love To Hate
Mel really hates 'New Age men', '1990s men' and men who feel they've got to be a stereotype. If men act like lads, that's okay as long as they're not doing it to be fashionable. But the ones she hates the most are those who are too caring – they make her sick! She also can't abide blokes who wait outside her house and knock on the window at three in the morning.
She wouldn't necessarily be attracted to a guy with a suit and a briefcase, even though he might be nice – she'd have to see the suit first! Vanity is another no-no: if her man didn't want to take a bath for a week that's all right with her, but if he was looking in the mirror at himself more than at her – that's bad.
Nat hates guys who wear pants that are supposed to be fitted but have gone all baggy. Blokes who dance like nerds on the dancefloor are also a real turn-off as far as she's concerned… she's outta there! It doesn't work when guys try to impress her either – she rates that a real turn off. Nic loathes name-droppers, while Shaznay hates men who can't make a decision and just go along with everything you say. Yes, Miss…!

Men They'd Love To Date
Shaznay, a real romantic, loves those loving, caring kinda guys – in fact, she admits she's never been out with anyone who's *not* romantic! She really likes a cuddle. She likes men who aren't scared to show their true feelings. If a guy isn't romantic when she's with him, our Shaz would immediately think

Shaznay, a real romantic, loves those loving, caring kinda guys.

Saints in Love

something was wrong. For her, it's the way a man carries himself – the way he comes across. Men might be really good looking, but if they don't approach it in the right way, that isn't cool.

Nic likes a guy who can blow her away with his confidence, and she likes it when they are very outgoing and successful in what they do. She likes men who can teach her something new. Nic likes older guys because they've got more savvy. She loves a man who can make her laugh, who can be really smart and has a good head on his shoulders. Nat adores men who are wise, while Mel fancies men who show a bit of style and know how to carry themselves.

All Saints Chat 'Em Up

Nic claims never to chat anyone up. She just flirts, because she thinks chatting up is 'ugly'. Nat confesses to having made a move on someone in a club and then falling down the stairs while he was watching. Not very cool…

Shaz reckons she and her boyfriend didn't chat each other up: they just started talking together. Mel was at a party recently where she chatted up a guy – but when he asked her for her number she came over all shy and spent the rest of the evening avoiding him!

Saucy Secrets

Nic remembers about three years ago Nat set her up on a blind date with the brother of Nat's current boyfriend. They went out for dinner and two days later she moved from London to Manchester to live with him. The bloke in question was called Darren, and to this day Nic's mum throws a wobbly if anybody mentions his name! Nic and he were together for about a year and she admits her whole life used to revolve around

Mel fancies men who show a bit of style and know how to carry themselves.

him… but she couldn't do that any more. Nat went out with a guy who thought he knew everything about girly things – brand names and so on. He once made a thing of pointing out a Gucci dress in a department store, but Nat's reaction was to send him off to his own department!

Mel confesses to having never experienced true love. What usually happens is that she falls completely for someone who doesn't love her.

All Saints Story - Part 2

For All Saints, hard work and good fortune came together when the musical climate changed almost overnight with the advent of the Spice Girls in the summer of 1996. Suddenly, being female was in and every record label in the phone book was looking out for its own version. All Saints were happy to take advantage of Girl Power – but certainly didn't want to be seen as carbon copies of the infamous five.

Indeed, All Saints chose their current record company, London, precisely because all the others they saw just wanted them to be replicas of Mel B, Mel C, Victoria, Emma and Geri. They even turned down record deals with big labels such as Sony, a courageous move for a bunch of girls desperate for success.

Shaznay reckons it showed far more Girl Power to wait until they were appreciated for their music. Mel, ever the business brain, explains that though making the music is incredibly personal and creative, it goes hand in hand with the politics and percentages that come with landing a record deal. Making good music isn't enough in itself. She admits that she found playing the field really frustrating when what they all really wanted to do was make music and get it out to the public.

Remember, though, that while the Spices came together in response to an advert in *The Stage*, the growth of All Saints from an idea to reality was much more of an organic process. Musically, too, there was no need to bury differences in a show of unity: they were all singing from the same hymn-sheet. All four shared the same musical influences,

All Saints Story Part 2

...the best demo tape in the world!

and were united in their ambition to land a deal for All Saints.

London Records' chairman Tracy Bennett was certainly sold on his new signings. He was confident that All Saints were going to be the biggest band in the world – and nothing that's happened since ink hit paper has caused him to change that view one bit. The girls were thrilled when they signed with London, partly because they were the first company to see All Saints as a unique group in their own right and partly because of London's calibre. The company had previously signed bands like Fine Young Cannibals and East 17 and had also had a lot of success with all-girl group Bananarama, the biggest all-female hitmakers of the 1980s.

London has always had a history of finding female acts and treating them with respect rather than as one-hit wonders. Bennett saw All Saints' potential and immediately signed them in November 1996. He admits though that it was his long-time friend (now All Saints manager) John Benson who first brought him a demo tape of the group, and he was initially reluctant to hear the tapes. Having done so, though, he was astounded at what he'd heard: six songs, all of them hit material. Little wonder he later described it as the best demo tape in the world! The record company boss couldn't believe his luck; he hadn't actively been looking for a new band to sign and now a great one had dropped on to his lap. He also says that, though he's dealt with many bands, Shaznay is by far the best songwriter he's ever worked with.

Having secured a record deal, the next step for All Saints was to record the album and release a single. The production team decided to enlist the help of Neneh Cherry and Massive Attack producer Cameron McVey, with further input from Karl Gordon, a famous DJ from the Steve Jervier stable, and Johnny Douglas, whose main claim to fame was working with George Michael. Though the group admire Neneh Cherry, they say her music isn't a big influence – but even so they have to admit husband Cameron McVey was fabulous to work with.

Nic

Full name: Nicole Marie Appleton

Nickname: Nic, Nici, the Fonz or Fonzie

Date of birth: 7 December 1975

Age: 22

Star sign: Sagittarius

Eyes: Brown

Distinguishing marks: She's got a tattoo of the Year of the Tiger symbol on her waist and a belly button ring

Lives: Camden, London

Likes: McDonald's

Dislikes: Dishonesty

Ambition: To design a new uniform for the police force

Life before All Saints: She was a waitress, hotel singer, bartender and lifeguard

Music that gets her buzzin': Nic really appreciates music and likes anything that's good, particularly hip-hop. But she also loves a good rock, current hot faves being the Prodigy and Oasis

Which Saint is she? Nic is the 'life and soul' of the group. She describes herself as sweet, easy-going and mad!

Saint or sinner? According to Nic, she's a saint who sins in a saintly way!

Perfect man: She reckons Liam Gallagher and George Clooney combined would be just about perfect! Nic likes a man to have a crazy side and also an older and more sophisticated side

Fave hunk: *ER*'s George Clooney

What the other Saints say: Nicole's the crazy one of the group

Earliest memory: She remembers Christmas morning in England when she was 8, walking into the kitchen and seeing her mum and older sister who had come over from New York to visit. She recalls it was such a shock, but fantastic!

Wickedest thing ever done: Nic once went out with two guys for a whole year! She was so clever at concealing one from the other they never found out

Nic once went out with two guys for a whole year!

Nic

Daredevil Nic is Mel's best friend both in and out of All Saints. She says she has an evil sense of humour, and there's nothing she wouldn't do for a laugh, provided nobody gets hurt. She first met Mel at school where they hung out, but lost touch when she went off with sister Nat to live in New York for a few years. Luckily she bumped into Mel on her return to England and was asked to join the group.

Nic went to school in Canada, where she was a cheerleader for the school football team called the Devils. Fame struck early for Nic when she was on the cover of the school magazine in her cheerleader outfit.

When she was 16 she wanted to find out about her Jewish faith (she is half Jewish) so she could understand what was happening at family gatherings. She doesn't practise a religion these days, however.

Nic and her sister Natalie are very close, and sometimes fancy the same guys. Occasionally she might look at a boy Nat's with, but she'd never do anything about it. Nic and Nat went out with two brothers for a while.

Her parents are very happy for her. She says her mum used to phone her from America all the time because she was worried Nic wasn't eating. In the beginning, when it was just Shaznay, Mel and Nic, they had nothing at all – they'd share Pot Noodles for dinner. Her parents stuck with her and had faith and now they're just as excited as she is.

She used to have a diary that she'd take to bed with her when she was younger. Now she can't live without her Walkman or her mobile phone.

Nic hasn't had a boyfriend for two years. She's got a crush on Robbie Williams but knows she hasn't got a chance as he goes for girls half her size! She also says she fancies Johnny Vaughan from the *Big Breakfast* and likes her men to have tattoos. Nic is scared of people knowing her true feelings, having been hurt before, and that is probably why she hasn't been involved for a while. It's nice for Nic and Mel that they are both in the same boat when it comes to guys.

Nic is the first to admit she's lazy and, if it's cold and raining outside, there's nothing she loves better than snuggling up inside with someone she likes. When she's on her own she just chills out, watches TV and does what she wants. She likes a good argument and getting things off her chest, but prefers arguing with guys because women are 'quite vicious' when they argue. She knows that sometimes she needs to be put in her place as she can be a bit bossy.

Nic's very proud of the band and loves reading about them in magazines: she also enjoys smiling for the cameras and reckons she's cut out for fame. An easy-going girl, she let people walk all over her when she was younger but now she stands up for herself. She thinks the music business is a scary one to be in. Right now, though, the music business is probably more scared of her!

Nic's Saintly Views

Nic on Mel
She's beautiful!

On food
She eats lots of crisps, especially Doritos.

On staying up all night
Nic and Mel once tried to stay up all night in New York by spooning mouthfuls of instant coffee washed down with Diet Coke. They didn't stay awake – they just felt sick!

On daft phrases
Nic's most used phrase is 'Gooomks!', which means a real wally.

On her favourite films
Grease and *Dirty Dancing* are Nic's favourites: she can watch them over and over again. She also loves *The Muppet Movie* and *The Usual Suspects*.

On a good night out
Nic's idea of a good night out is any one of her recent birthdays; they were perfect and she could go mad with her family and friends. Nic also likes being with people, especially ones who are down to earth and can have a good laugh and a gossip.

On being scared witless
Nic gets scared by rapists, murderers and horrible people. She can't watch programmes like *Crimewatch*. She's half Jewish, and ignorance like racism scares her too!

On success
Success has changed Nic in little ways. She used to get freaked out by meeting so many celebrities – but when you become an artist you realize these people are actually normal.

On holidays
When she was small, Nic used to go on holiday to Cornwall in a turquoise caravan. When it was parked outside the house after their return, she and her friends would use it like a Wendy House.

On doing the laundry
She does her own when she's got time – otherwise she gets her mum to help her. She wouldn't want someone else going through her knickers!

On the Spice Girls
Nic liked the Spice Girls' singles 'Say You'll Be There' and 'Spice Up Your Life', but thinks the rest of their music is rather light. She reckons if they met up they'd get on okay, though.

Nic and Mel once tried to stay up all night in New York by spooning mouthfuls of instant coffee washed down with Diet Coke

Fame and Fashion!

All Saints On Fame

Fame and fortune is what most pop stars strive for – but how does it change their lives? All Saints give us the low-down on the highs and lows of fame…

Nat says she first realized they were famous when she saw a huge billboard of the group in London's Shepherd's Bush.

Nic says they even have to wear hats and sunglasses to go to the shops now!

Shaznay complains they never have *time* to shop.

Mel has gained a lot more confidence in herself.

Nic says it's extremely gruelling when they are away because people do things very differently. In Japan, the fans go crazy and cry in front of them!

Nic reckons people ask a lot of questions but nobody has treated them like aliens yet. Other artists treat her differently. **Nat** says their friends don't treat them any differently but strangers act weird.

Shaznay doesn't like the spotlight because it makes her wary of everyone.

When it come to mixing a love life and fame, **Mel** says they have to be discreet.

Nat reckons it's more acceptable for girl bands to have boyfriends than boy bands girlfriends because the girls get jealous of the boys' girls. Got that?

Nic says they even have to wear hats and sunglasses to go to the shops now!

Fame and fashion!

All Saints On Fashion

All Saints like to look good, and favour the casual look that's easy to wear like army trousers, Nike trainers, casual jackets and slinky tops. They buy their gear from a variety of places like Kensington Market, DKNY, Topshop, Diesel and Hennes.

Shaznay is a real bargain hunter when it comes to clothes, and recently bought a green jacket from a camping shop on London's Oxford Street; it only cost her a fiver!

Nat has a penchant for baggy trousers and comfortable clothes and really loves Diesel gear. But when she's going out for the evening she likes to dress up in leather mini-skirts and look a bit more glamorous.

Nic and **Nat** share clothes.

Nic has a passion for army stuff, even if it's been around for years. She loves trainers too. But when she goes out in the evening she enjoys wearing slick suits.

Mel loves her leather coat because it's really comfortable and she can wear it anywhere. Mel nearly lost a Diesel jacket she bought in Japan at the MTV Awards. She left it there and they said they couldn't find it… but when she went back a month later it was exactly where she'd left it!

Calvin Klein is one of **Shaznay**'s favourite designers because his clothes are really nice without being over the top. She also likes hanging out in comfortable stuff like combat trousers, because she loves to slouch!

Shaznay also likes hanging out in comfortable stuff like combat trousers, because she loves to slouch!

All Saints Story – Part 3

The album *All Saints* was primarily recorded at Matrix and Metropolis studios, with a short session in Washington after a lot of blood, sweat and tears from everybody involved. Twelve tracks were committed to recording tape – ten new songs and a couple of choice cover versions – of which more later. Now it was time to select a track to launch All Saints into the competitive music world. As if you didn't already know, the debut single chosen was 'I Know Where It's At'.

Amazingly for a first record that sounds so fresh and contemporary it could have been penned yesterday, 'I Know…' was actually co-written by Shaznay more than 4 years ago! Produced by Cameron McVey, it features mixes from Cutfather and Jo and a short rap by Shaznay. The single was released in the UK on 18 August 1997 and the girls immediately hit the promotional trail to push it, including an appearance on breakfast television at what was an unearthly hour for most of them! Thankfully, the camera appeared to fall in love with All Saints straightaway, and record shops were inundated with requests for the new single from 'that great girl group we saw on the box'. If the summer of '96 had seen the Spices surf to fame on a sunshine wave, it was clear from the outset that summer '97 would be the season of All Saints!

The song had legs, too, reaching Number 4 in the UK charts (in which it hung around for eight weeks) and Number 1 in Japan. Three months later, they opted to release a sultry love tune, 'Never Ever', as the next single. The change of pace was a daring move, but a shrewd one: even though the downbeat feel was light years away from the sunnily optimistic debut, it was to prove even more of a resounding success. Written by Shaznay, the song reflects a very personal and tumultuous period in her's and Mel's lives, when they were both suffering from the distressing effects of relationship break-ups. Nic remembers when Shaznay first wrote 'Never Ever' and brought it round to her house: she told the girls to learn it, and they all loved it immediately. They thought it would do well in the charts, but had no idea just how well. Maybe it caught the change of mood from autumn to winter just as 'I Know…' had captured sunshine in its grooves. Whatever, the song just didn't seem to know when to quit, and by mid-January 1998 had climbed to Number 1.

The success of All Saints' second single also had another effect. Its very different style

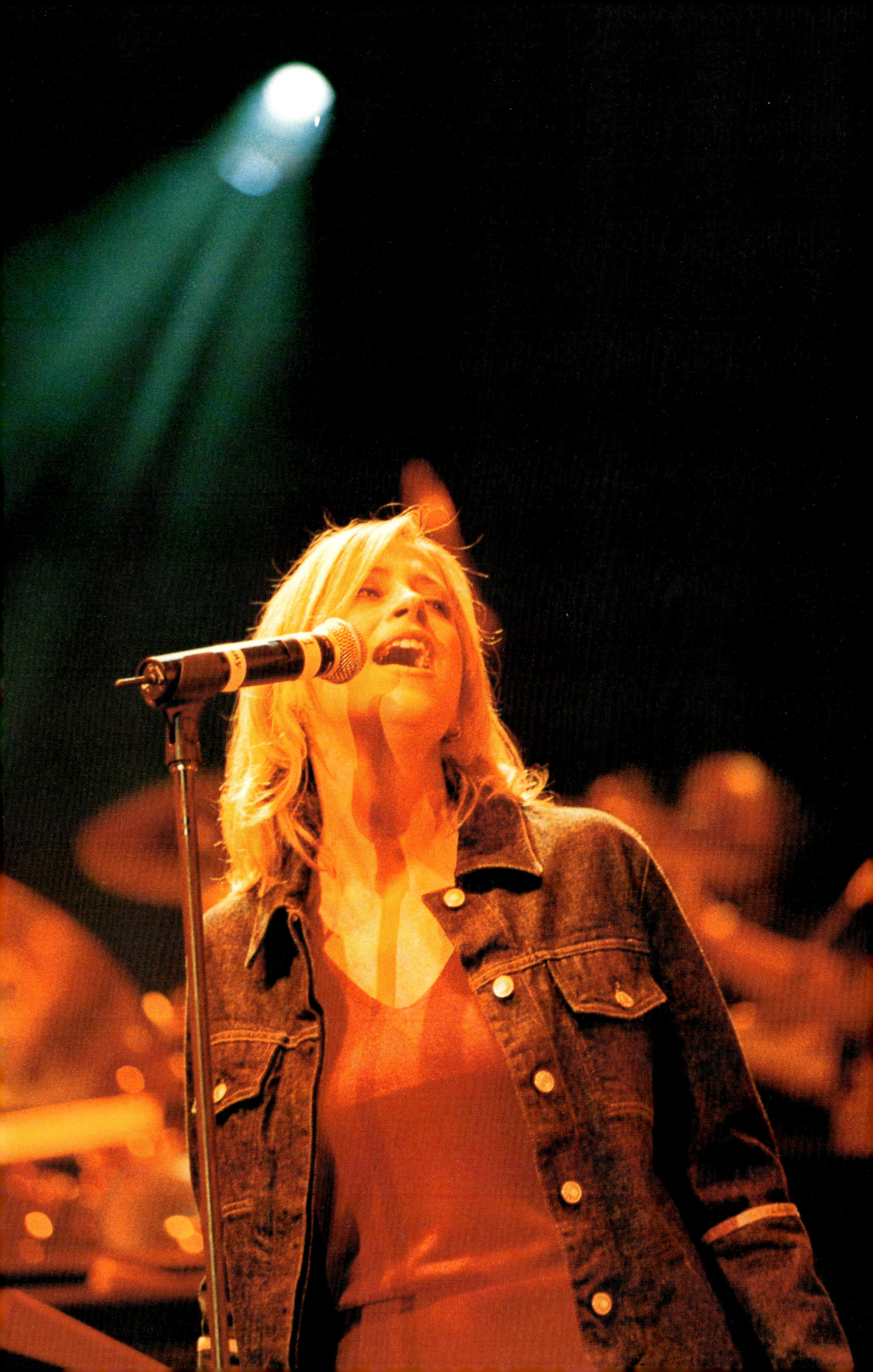

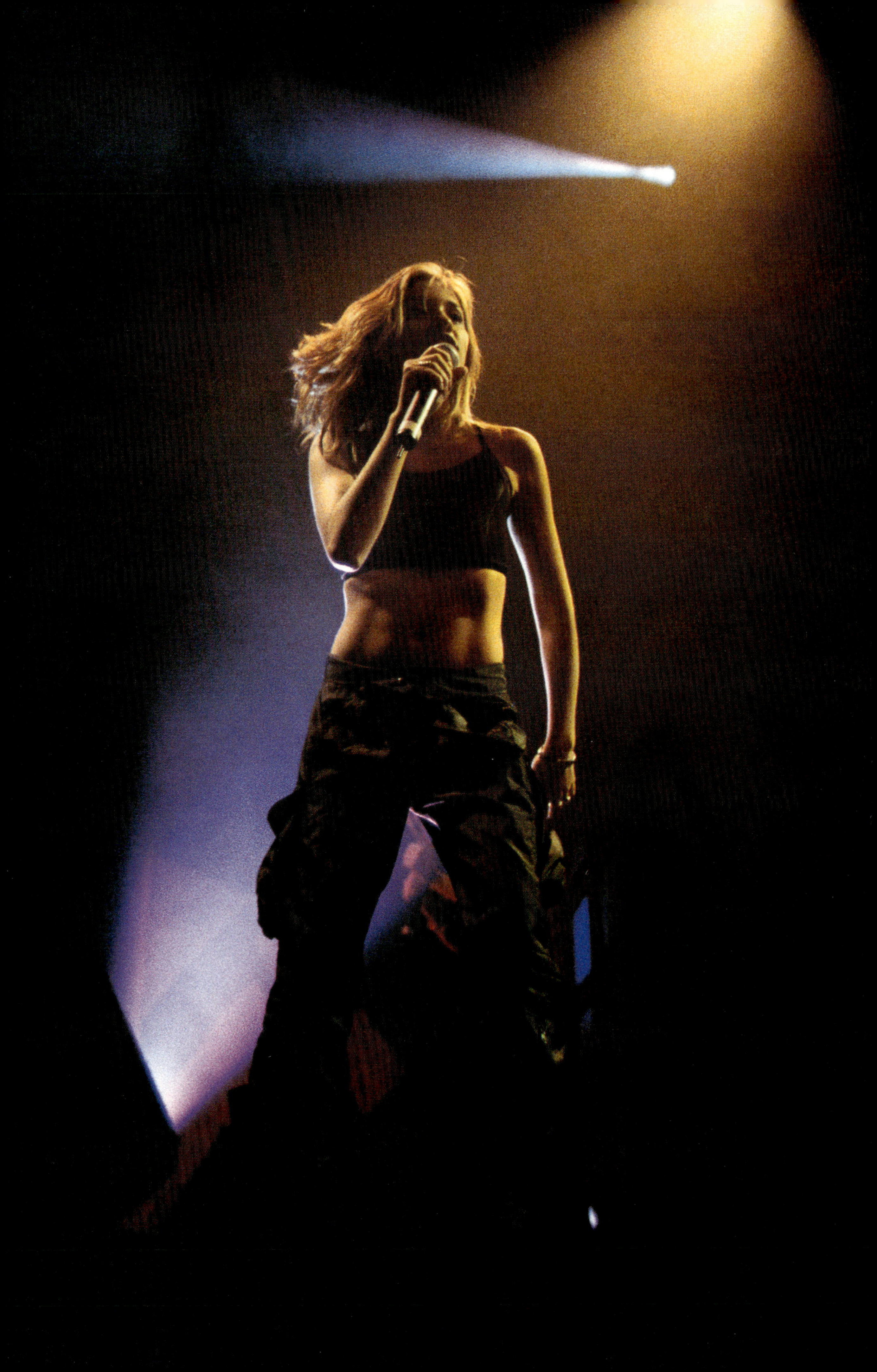

All Saints Story - Part 3

> A mere five months earlier, the four lasses who make up All Saints were complete unknowns – now everyone was talking about them.

showed the girls had the talent to produce more than just dance music; that as well as appealing to the teenage audience they could captivate an older audience too. And that proved a Godsend when the album, also named *All Saints*, was released in November. Mel describes it as slow and groove-based, while critics describe it as offering a fresh twist on En Vogue and the Spice Girls. Whatever, *All Saints* shot up the charts and in mid-January 1998 it reached Number 2 in the charts. Considering it was up against the Girl Power marketing machine that was no mean achievement!

A mere five months earlier, the four lasses who make up All Saints were complete unknowns – now everyone was talking about them. Let's take a look behind the scenes…

Shaznay, the songwriter, is the quiet one of the group, slow to come out of her shell. She wants her music to be taken seriously, and so she should. Mel is the cynic of the group; she organizes the others and it's to her they run if they need medicinal help – she carries everything from aspirins to gum in her bag. Nic's the practical joker, always mucking about: she'll do anything for a dare. At the grand old age of 24, sister Natalie's the eldest – the one with a level head on her shoulders.

Make no mistake: these are four bright women. They all have educational qualifications of some kind and have the same goals. That's to produce great music and stay around for a long, long time… a philosophy echoed by their record company. London are intent on bringing on the girls slowly and building on their success.

The company's marketing department has been painfully aware of the obvious comparisons between All Saints and the Spice Girls, and have taken steps to build the group in a credible fashion. Their marketing director, Laurie Cokell, believes they have more in common with bands like TLC, En Vogue and other R&B-based bands, and in keeping with this 'serious' approach their first press coverage was not in the tabloids or teen mags but in *The Face*, the band being presented as streetwise rather than up front and sassy. Manager John Benson insists All Saints are being treated as an act with a long shelf-life. Their third single from the album, released in February 1998, was a cover of 'Lady Marmalade' – a US chart-topper in 1975 for US soul trio LaBelle – while the other non-original song, the Red Hot Chili Peppers' 'Under The Bridge', seemed a strong candidate to follow it up. Whichever single they chose to put out, there was no question of it being anything but a hit. It seems right now that everything they touch turns to pure gold. As ever, All Saints knew precisely where it's at – and that's where they are right now…

Nat

Heartbreaker Natalie admits she gets tired of boyfriends quickly and thinks nothing of dumping them

Full name: Natalie Jane Appleton

Nickname: Nat or Fat Cat, because she was a chubby baby!

Date of birth: 14 May 1973

Age: 24

Star sign: Taurus

Eyes: Hazel

Distinguishing marks: None

Lives: Camden, London, with her dad

Likes: Stephen King stories that scare you witless

Dislikes: Flying. She hates it when the plane takes off as she always wonders how a great big thing like a plane is gonna get up there?

Ambition: For people to appreciate All Saints' music and their individuality

Life before All Saints: She used to teach aerobics and sing in bars and once had a bit part in *Grange Hill*

Music that gets her buzzin': Nat likes a real mixture of music like a lot of old ballads, old school rap and American classic rock

Earliest memory: Natalie was thrilled when she went to Disneyworld when she was really young. She couldn't wait to meet Snow White and the Seven Dwarfs. She reckoned it was the best thing ever to happen to her!

Which Saint is she? Nat would like to think she's the leader of the group… and knows it! She confesses she bosses everyone around like a big sister and describes herself as friendly, outgoing and impatient

Saint or sinner? Heartbreaker Natalie admits she gets tired of boyfriends quickly and thinks nothing of dumping them. Overall, though, she reckons she learns from her mistakes and although she admits to doing some naughty things she's turned out a better person for it

Perfect man: Her perfect guy would be Brad Pitt because he's quiet and really down to earth. Nat says Brad is really gorgeous and, though she doesn't usually go for guys that all the girls like, she makes an exception for Brad because he's amazing!

What the other Saints say: Nat's the 'bossy boots' of the group

Fave hunk: Brad Pitt – see above!

Wickedest thing ever done: Nat once kissed a friend's boyfriend when she was in the next room!

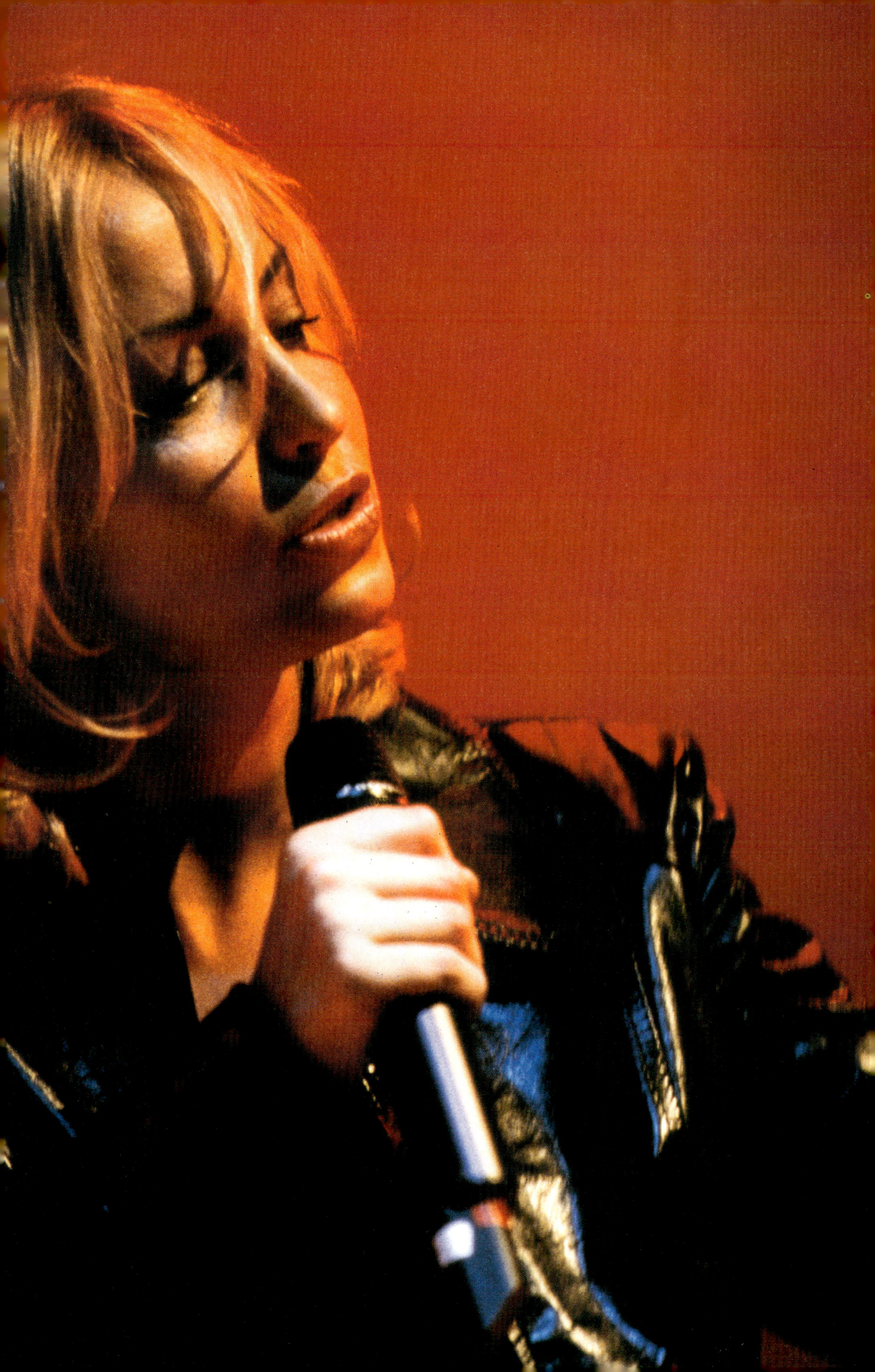

Profile

Nat

Natalie's the eldest in the group and was the last to join All Saints. She admits to being their Number 1 fan right from the start and she knew all the words to their songs already, so didn't have to learn them when she joined!

Like Nic and Mel, she went to the Sylvia Young Theatre School and has always enjoyed being up there in the limelight. At 15, she had her mother dress her up so she could sing in New York bars and she confesses no one knew how young she was. She used to sing in bars for people of all ages: one minute she'd be singing 'Tie A Yellow Ribbon', the next she'd be strutting around like Madonna! She became the school 'babe' and she showed off a bit: she once dyed her hair and pretended to be a pop star.

She's quite close to her sister but confesses Nic doesn't tell her any big secrets because she gets too emotional. Natalie used to play all sorts of practical jokes on Nic, but her little sister is old enough now to get her own back. She takes out her frustration on her mum and, if she's annoyed at the group, she shouts at Nic. She says you can always take things out on the people you're closest to. She always apologizes afterwards, though! She reckons she's a bit heartless when it comes to relationships and always ends up hurting people.

Nat admits she gets bored with men quickly and her relationships never seem to last longer than three months. She was hurt really badly by a boyfriend once when she was younger, which has coloured her approach to relationships now. She has been in love since then but simply doesn't become emotionally attached any more. But that doesn't stop men falling at her feet... With her sophisticated looks and effortless charm, guys are putty in her hands and she knows just how to put them under her spell. She's had a fling with someone famous, but her lips are firmly sealed as to that person's identity.

Nat speaks her mind most of the time, but admits that sometimes you have to put on a pretty face and smile, especially in the music business – though she finds it hard to pretend because she's a terrible liar! Down to earth, honest and real is how she describes herself, but she confesses she's very stubborn and has a quick temper and no patience. She gets really angry with people ahead of her in the queue who try to pay for a pair of socks by credit card, and *hates* traffic jams! She always has to have her own way and will argue to the death about something because she always thinks she's right. She is untidy but obsessed with cleanliness. She hates it if someone cooks her something without washing their hands first – she just can't eat it. Natalie nearly became All Saints' manager because she thought she'd be better at wheeling and dealing, but decided to join the group instead. She's never been happier and is glad she did. So are we!

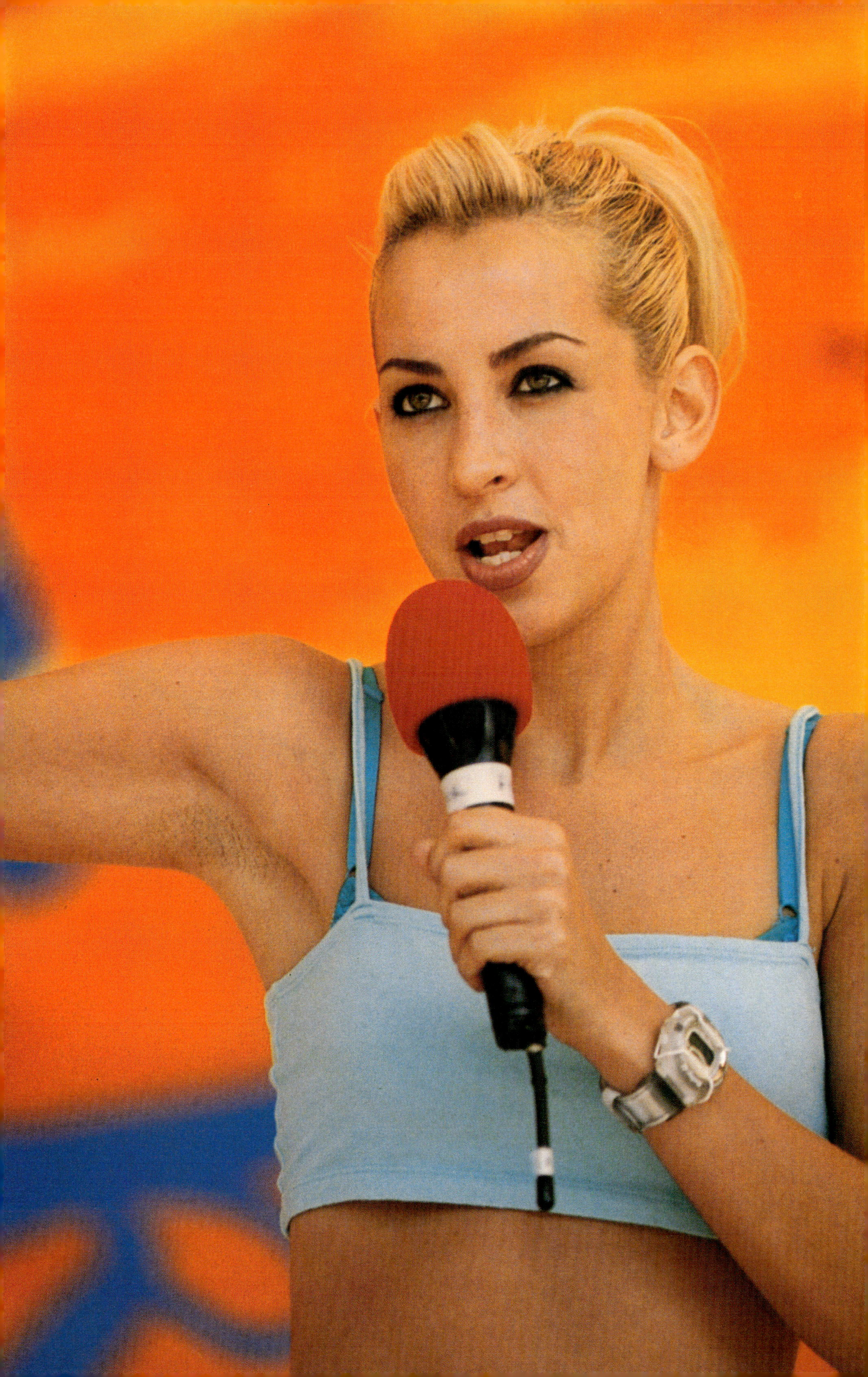

Nat's Saintly Views

On Nic
Nat says she loves her sister to bits… but they used to fall out when she tried to interfere with her boyfriends because she thought they weren't good enough.

On life without
Nat can't live without her moisturiser cream, her hair brush, books, shades, Game Gear (which she nicked from her brother-in-law), a photo of Brad Pitt, and her family.

On favourite films
Nat loves films – especially *Some Like It Hot*, *Goodfellas* and *Dirty Dancing* which she says are cool.

On a good night out
Nat's favourite night out is to start with a long bath and go for a meal with a nice guy. After that she'd go out to meet some friends at a bar for a drink. Perfect!

On the importance of fame
Natalie may be in a group that's heading for global recognition, but she doesn't think it's important to be famous – though she *does* think it's important to receive recognition for her music.

On flirting
When it comes to flirting with new men Natalie's in her element. She says she's a pro. So what's her best tip? Slant your mouth, squint your eyes and smile – it *really* works!

On a good night in
On a night in, Natalie likes nothing better than being with someone she's really in love with, a huge bottle of wine and *Scream* on video. Nat likes staying in on Friday night because everyone else goes out.

On herself
Natalie isn't scared of failure as long as she's given it her best shot. She's a bit of a perfectionist. She says her worst habits are belching and not tidying her room.

Nat can't live without her moisturiser cream, her hair brush, books, shades, Game Gear, a photo of Brad Pitt, and her family.

felix blow

Saints or Sinners?

When it comes to being wicked All Saints are no angels. They may look naughty but are they really nice? Do they talk dirty just in their songs or should they be reaching for the soap to wash out their mouths when they're not performing? Saints or sinners? Devils or angels? Read on and judge for yourself…

SINNER
Mel says they can all be cheeky and that she'd fight anyone.

SAINT
Natalie loves lying in bed with her two cats Nathan and Nathana and is always having to clean up their mess!

SINNER
Nic has been stopped by the police twice: her advice for when this happens is to wind the window down and flutter your eyelashes. She was once pulled over in America by a cop who simply told her she should lock her door. She reckons the American police uniform is much sexier than the British one!

SINNERS
All Saints once broke into Public Demand's hotel room when they were performing away and completely wrecked the place. They squeezed toothpaste all up the walls and wrote 'All Saints woz 'ere!' They tore their bedclothes off the beds and trashed everything in sight. Shaznay admits they 'smashed it'. They got their comeuppance though – Public Demand got revenge by soaking them with a fire hose!

SAINT
When Nat was at school she really loved sport: as well as being the best runner she was really good at hockey because she used to beat people around the legs with her hockey stick! She was a real tough cookie. She abandoned the game in favour of ballet and explains that smashed up ankles and ballet just don't go together.

SINNERS
Mel rather guiltily admits to bullying a girl at stage school. When the poor girl turned up for sports day wearing a T-shirt with teddybears sewn all over it, they laughed like mad. Nic was suspended for a week for stealing a bag of crisps from the girl and Mel skived off to keep her company.

Nic was once pulled over in America by a cop who simply told her she should lock her door…

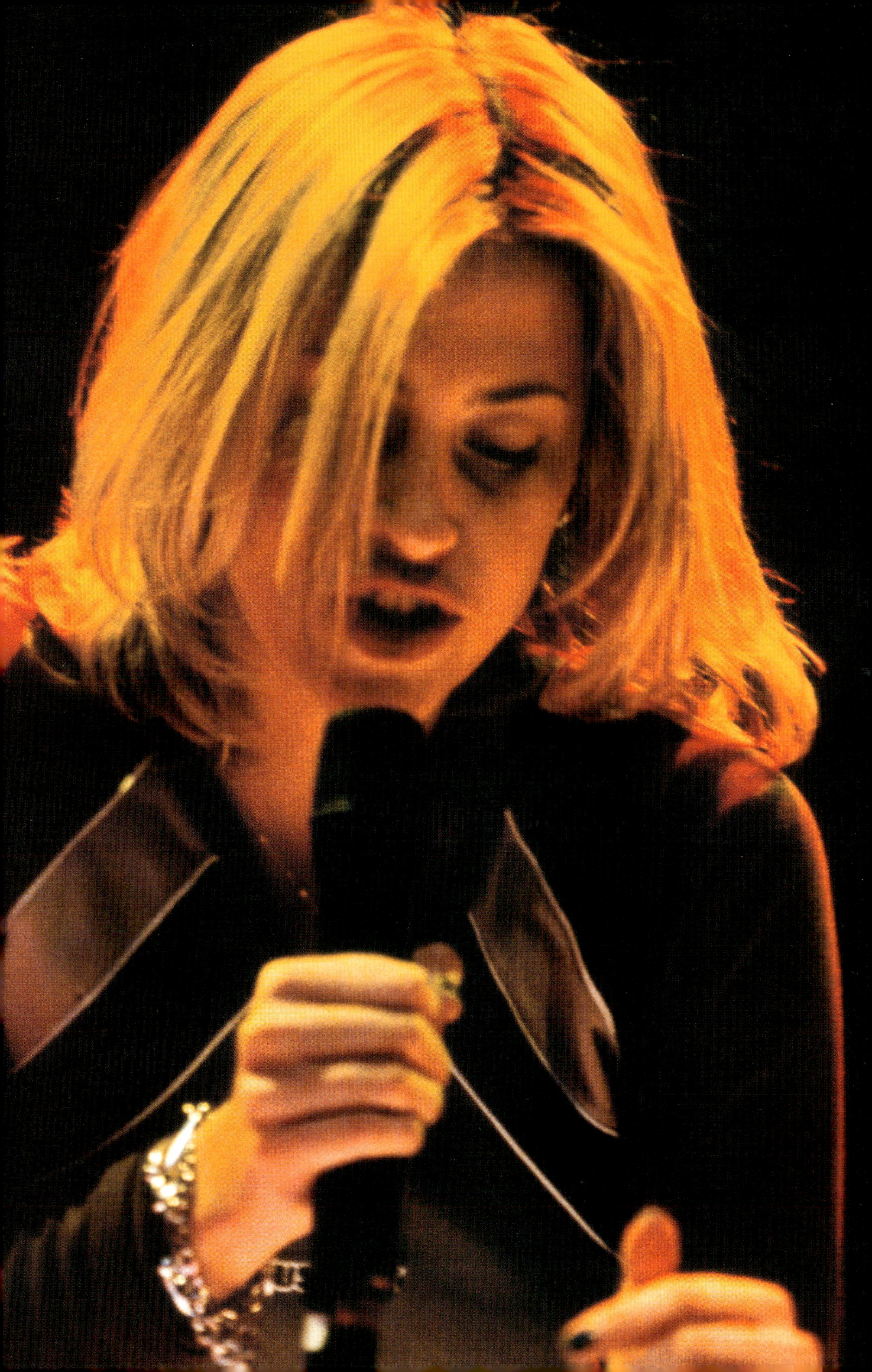

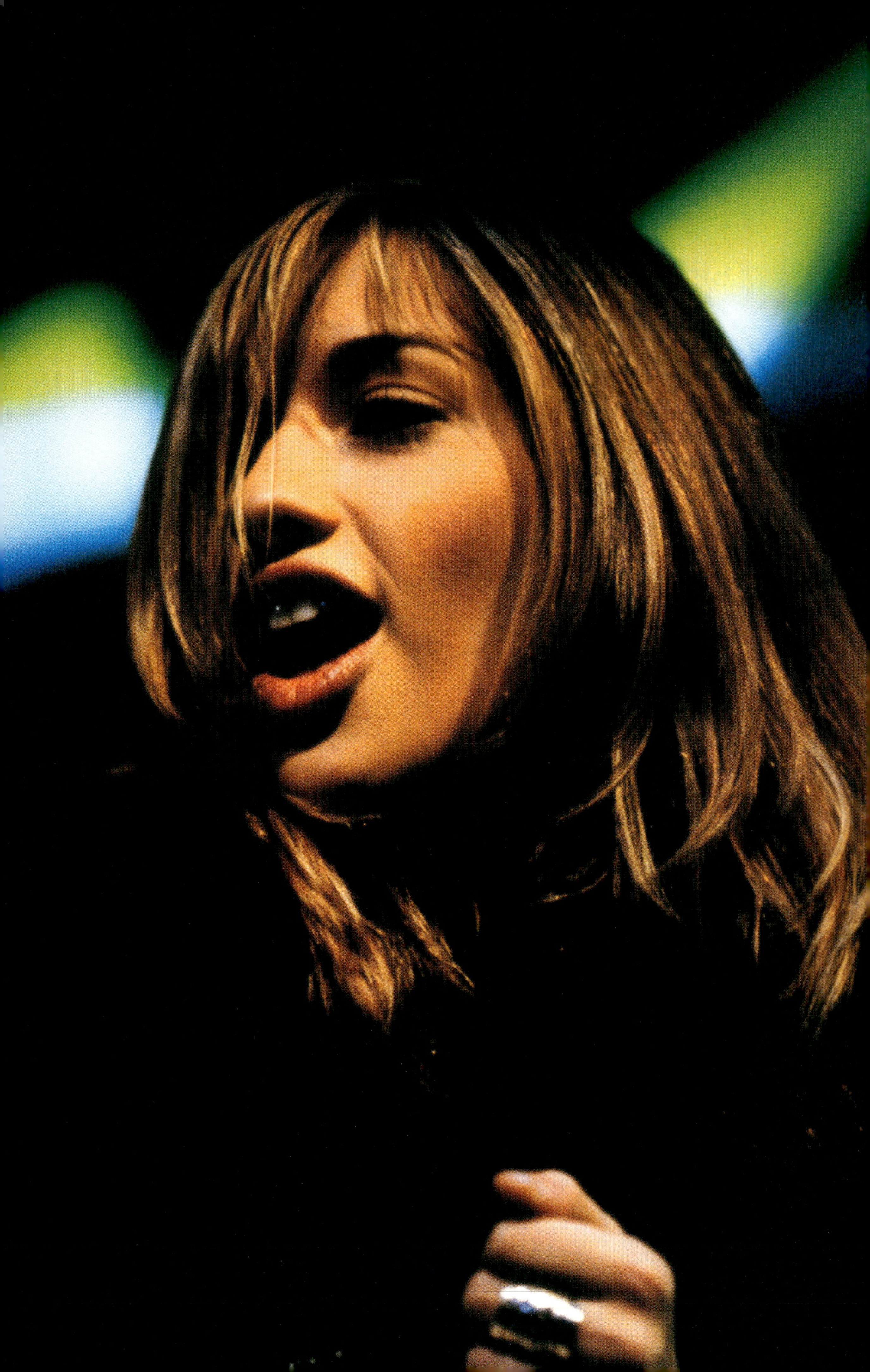

Saints or Sinners?

SAINT
Shaznay's mum is the most important person in her life and she's very protective towards her.

SINNER
Nat and Mel burst into Nic's and Shaznay's hotel room and threw wet cloths at them at two in the morning. The girls were not best pleased.

SAINT
Shaznay's got five GCSEs, namely Photography (she once took a picture inside a tree and developed it herself), Media Studies, English, Music and Art.

SINNER
Nic's older sister Nat decided to scalp her with a pair of garden shears when she was little. Nic remembers she had really long hair at the time and Nat decided it would be fun to cut it all off. Their parents went ballistic when they saw the almost bald Nic. They made her wear hats for months while it grew back and Nat got into *heaps* of trouble!

SAINT
Natalie maintains that the girls' families are the most important thing to all of them and that they all keep in close contact with their mums wherever they are.

SAINT AND SINNER
Mel used to have parties all the time when her parents were away, but always got caught out. Once her mum and dad went to Rotterdam for a weekend, leaving her in charge, and she had a huge party. She spent all day clearing up and made the house look spick and span… but when her mum came back she was furious because someone had been sick on the front door step. Poor old Mel hadn't thought to look outside!

> Nic's older sister Nat decided to scalp her with a pair of garden shears when she was little.

SINNER
Apparently things were once stolen from Nat's parents' house while she was having a party… which took some nifty explaining on Naughty Nat's part!

SAINT
Nic is a bit of whizz at putting on duvet covers and fluffing pillows, after being taught by a maid in America.

SINNER
Everyone accuses Nat of being bitchy… especially Nic!

SINNER
Nic once told everyone she was at home catching up on sleep when she was really out partying.

SINNER
When Mel's mum first saw her tattoo she gave her a piece of her mind.

SAINT
Shaznay's parents don't mind her having parties when they're there… or even when they're away.

SINNERS
Mel confesses she'd cheat on a bloke, especially if it was to be with Brad Pitt. Nat and Nic agree they'd cheat, too!

SAINT
Shaznay would never cheat on a guy, and thinks the others are awful for saying they would.

SAINT
Nat is a protective big sister. She used to get uptight with Nic as soon as she started dating a guy, but now lets her do her own thing and learn from her mistakes. She says she *dies* when someone makes Nic cry.

SINNER
Shaznay once binned a nightie her mum had bought her. She was in hospital two years ago with a stomach infection and her mum brought in all her things except for her PJs, so she gave her a frilly, flowery nightie with matching nightgown to wear. When the rest of the girls came to visit her she refused to get out of bed because she was too embarrassed. When the nurse came round she sent them all to the day room because they were making too much noise. Needless to say, the rest of the girls fell about at the sight of the nightie and still rib her about it now.

SINNER
Nic walks around the house with nothing on if she feels like it.

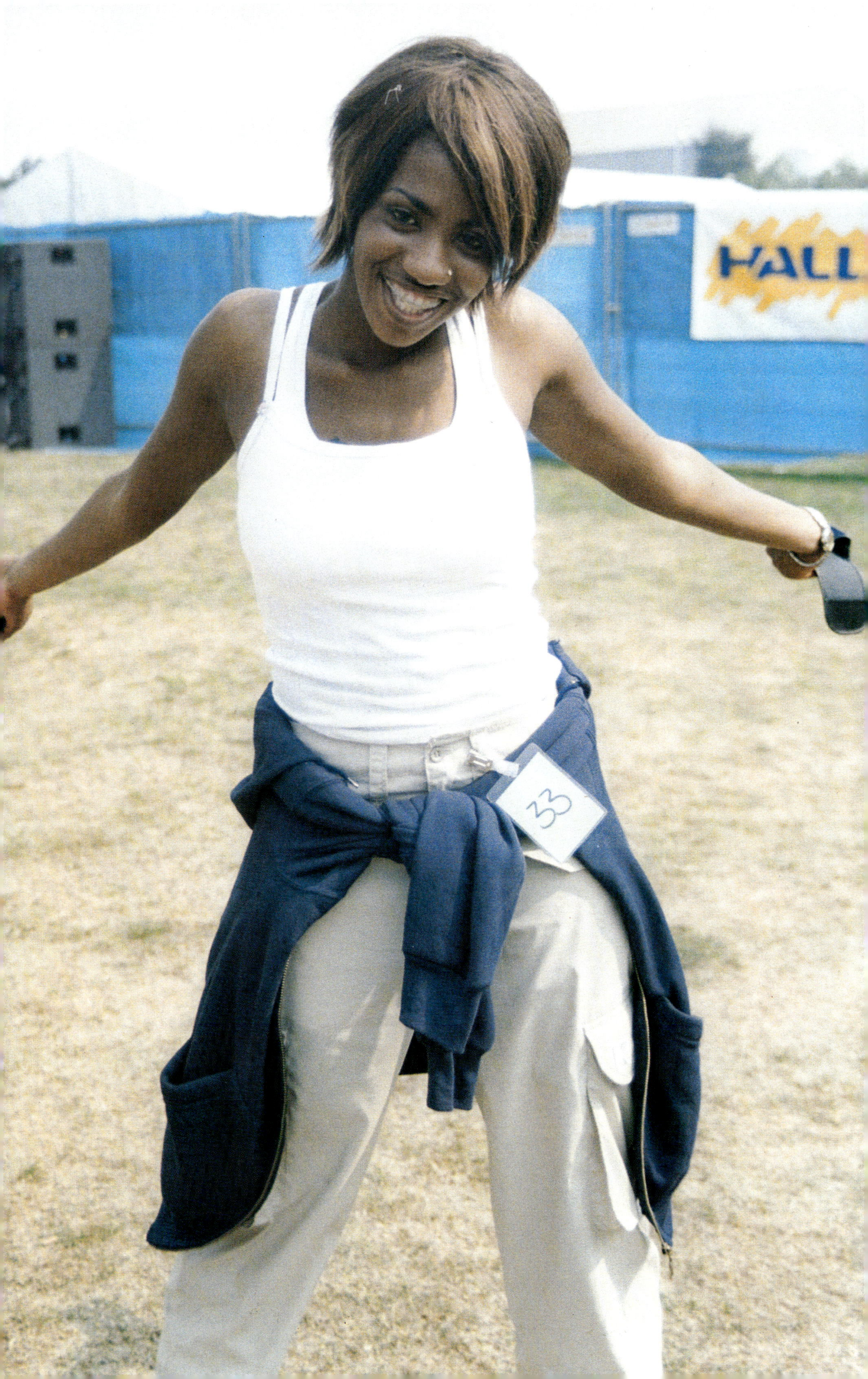
HALL
33

Shaznay

Full name: Shaznay Tricia Lewis

Nickname: Bart – because all her mates think she sounds like Bart Simpson when she raps

Date of birth: 14 October 1975

Age: 22

Star sign: Libra

Eyes: Brown

Distinguishing marks: Pierced nose and metal braces. She's also got a tattoo of the Year of the Rabbit symbol on her right breast

Lives: Islington, London, with her mum

Likes: Open-minded people and people who show respect

Dislikes: Rudeness

Ambition: For All Saints to be appreciated purely for their musical talents

Music that gets her buzzin': Shaz is a big rap fan and loves Missy Elliott who she says is really cool

Which Saint is she? Shaznay's the quiet, shy one of the group. She can be a bit of a nutter like the others but is usually the level-headed one

Saint or sinner? Shaznay admits to enjoying being a bit naughty even though she's quite religious. Verdict: probably a sinner

Perfect man: Shaznay likes Robert De Niro but isn't hooked on any one guy. Whoever he is, he would have to be somebody she could bond with and have loads of fun with

What the other Saints say: She's the sexiest one in the group

Earliest memory: Naughty Shaz recalls passing her driving test. When her examiner told her she's passed, she was so pleased she kissed him!

Wickedest thing ever done: Shaznay once crashed a friend's car… and then blamed it on someone else. To make up for her sins she did pay for the damage

Fave hunk: Brad Pitt. According to her, Brad's delicious!

Closely guarded secret: She once walked out of a loo in a night-club with her skirt tucked in her knickers!

Shaznay once crashed a friend's car… and blamed it on someone else

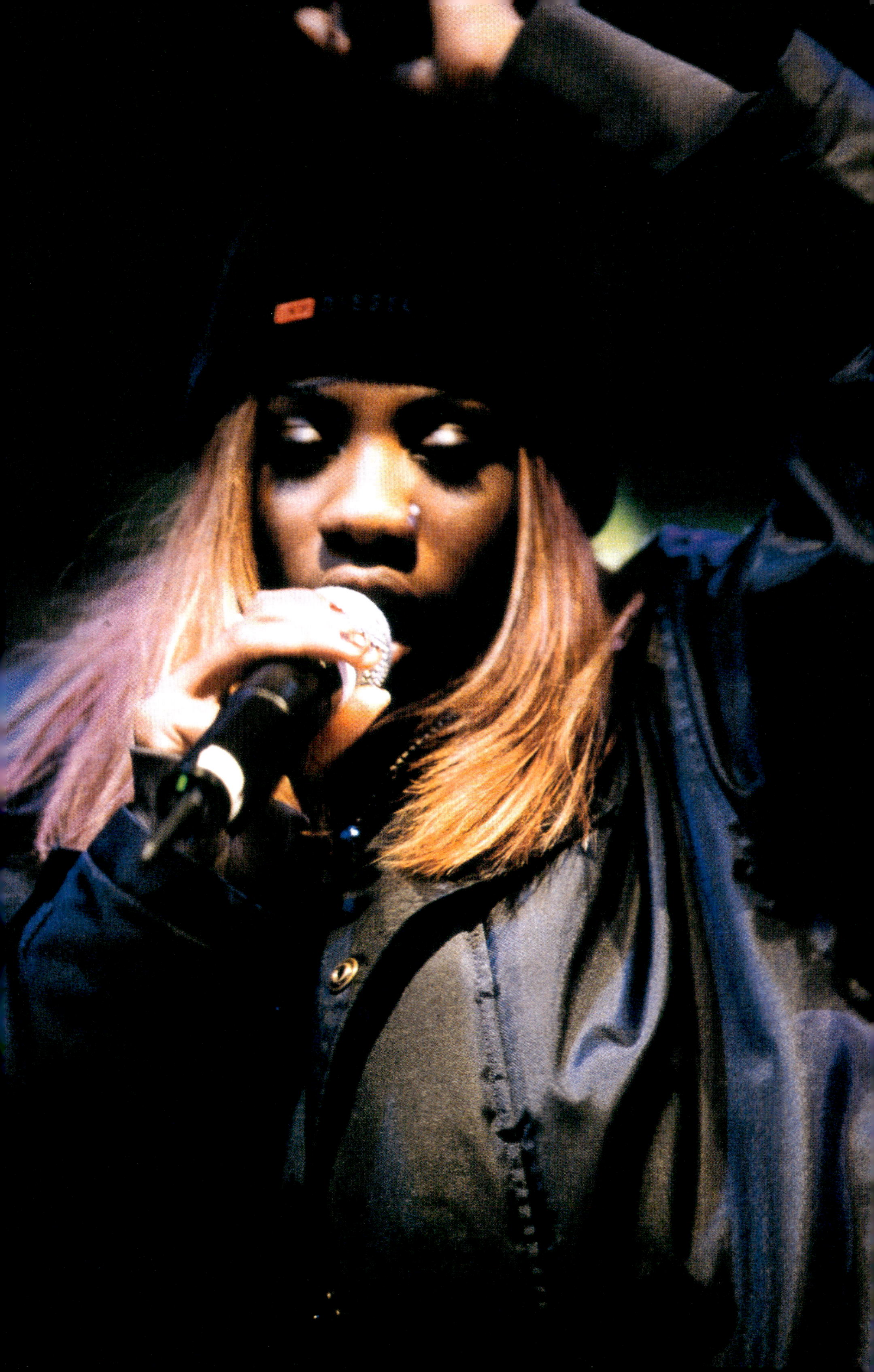

Shaznay

Shaznay T. Lewis is the songwriter of the group – she's sexy, warm, funny and very bright. She's also serious and quiet, but beneath that exterior lurks a wicked sense of humour. Her family and her music are her biggest passions, and she's fiercely protective of both. She adores her mum and says she has always been supportive. She's got a sister called Elaine who's 12 years older than her. They've only ever had one big row where they didn't speak for ages and their mum had to get them together again. Her sister is shy like her mum, but Shaz reckons she's the loud and outgoing one.

Before she went out with her first boyfriend Shaz was a real tomboy and hated kissing boys. She's had a 4-year relationship but is realistic about love these days – she never thinks it's going to last for ever. She'd like to get married and have children one day. Most of her friends are boys, mainly because she gets on better with them.

Though people sometimes criticize Shaznay for being hard, she says she isn't – even though she doesn't always smile when she meets people. She says she just doesn't go out of the way to open up. When Shaz is doing interviews she's quite serious because she doesn't want people to label the band as silly girls messing around. Once people have seen the serious side and start respecting the girls for their music *then* she'll mess around! If she wasn't with the band Shaz says she's be singing on her own. She has always wanted to do what she's doing now: her life revolves around music, that's what she's all about.

Her favourite place in the world is at home, slobbing out in front of the telly. Her favourite book is *Sleepers*: she says it's better than the film – *wicked*! She can't live without her mobile phone, but confesses the only famous person's number she's got on it is Shane's from Boyzone.

Shaz says she thinks that because she's a Libra she always weighs up both sides of an argument and is fair. She's very cautious before she goes ahead with anything, looking at all the possibilities first. She threw caution to the wind, though, when she dyed her hair blonde and it was a *disaster* – it kept going lighter and lighter so she had to dye it black, and these days leaves it to the professionals.

Don't be deceived by that 'holier than thou' exterior, though – she may look like butter wouldn't melt in her mouth, but we know differently! When asked what her idea of a good night out would be, Shaznay joked she'd like to take a whole week off so she could have fun knowing she'd not have to get up for four days! She'd go for a meal, go clubbing – the lot. That's Shaznay for you.

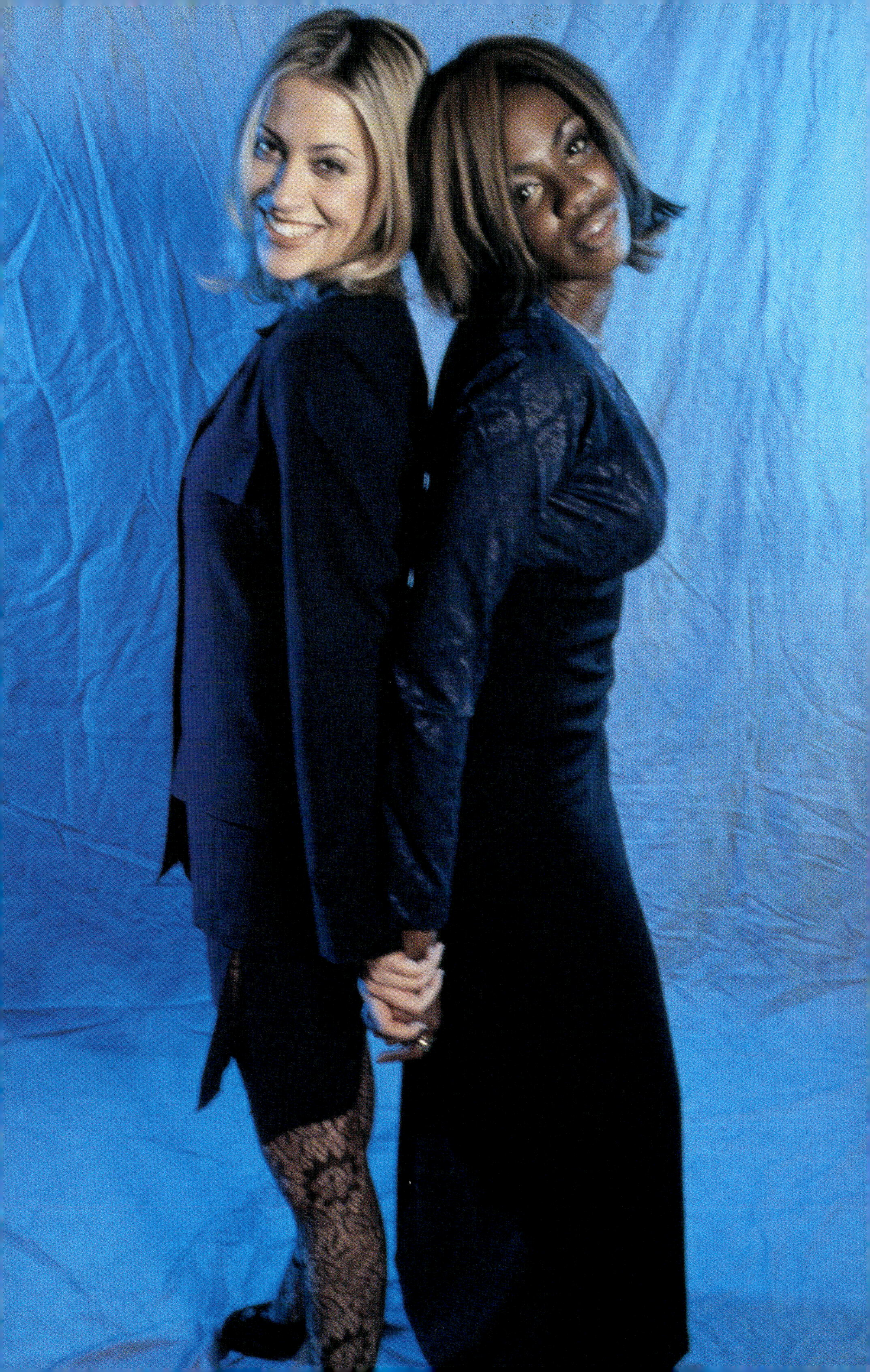

Shaznay's Saintly Views

Shaznay on Nat
She keeps us in line.

On her sexy lyrics
She thinks they're funny because they're explicit – and they rhyme!

On religion
Though Shaznay is Catholic, she doesn't have time to go to church these days.

On the press
When Shaznay went to a party with Boyz II Men, whom she's known for over five years, they had this big reunion because she hadn't seen them for ages and the papers said she was dating Wanya! She was so embarrassed…

On the rich and famous
Shaz says she's met loads of celebrities who were really nice and she reckons she would snog one or two of them – but she won't reveal who.

On doing the laundry
Shaznay says if All Saints are in the same hotel for a week they get room service to do the washing for them.

On football
Shaznay played for an Arsenal girls' football team, but admits they never went to any practice sessions and were so bad they never won a game. She wishes there had been an Arsenal badminton team, because she's a bit special at that!

On a good night in
Slouching in her front room covered in loads of blankets and duvets with a close friend is Shaznay's idea of a good night in. She'd have every remote control within easy reach and loads of food and drink! She loves staying in on a Friday night, because the TV's 'brilliant'.

On life without
Shaznay can't live without her deodorant, lots of underwear, shades and travel bottles of cosmetics.

On favourite films
Shaznay's favourite films include *Dumb and Dumber* and *The Usual Suspects*.

On her favourite expressions
Shaznay's most used expressions are 'For real' and 'Can you cope?'.

On Peter Andre
She thinks Peter is a nice guy but she doesn't fancy him. If he asked her out, she'd tell him she was washing her hair.

Shaznay played for an Arsenal girls' football team, but admits they never went to any practice sessions

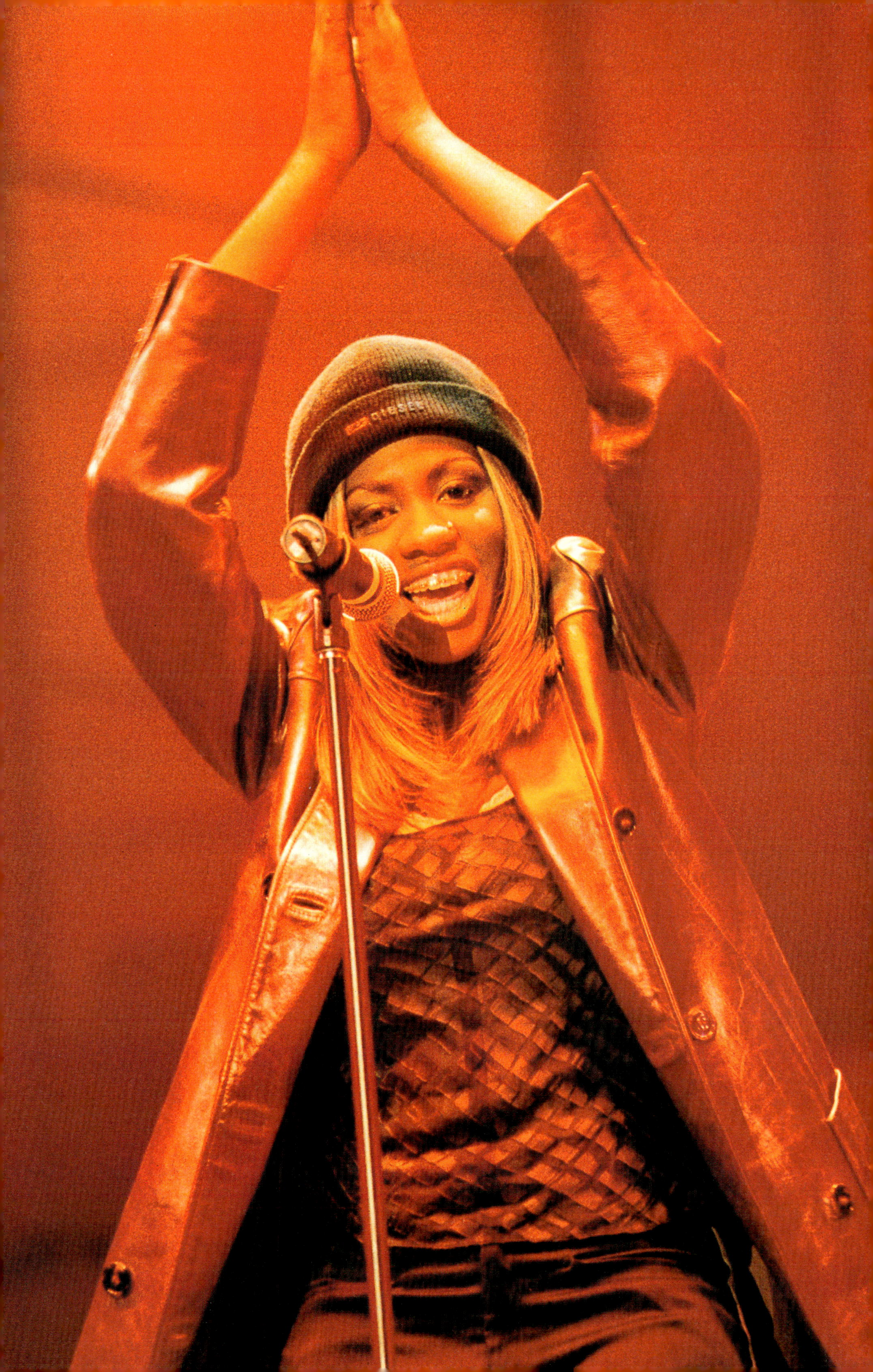

A-Z of All Saints

Some of the things you've always wanted to know about these wicked pop sensations… in strictly A for All Saints alphabetical order!

A is for **All Saints**, the name of the band that's funking its way to fame featuring four talented songwriters and vocalists who are sexy and smart to boot. It's also the name of their new album that's frothing with groovy tracks and littered with great lyrics. And, as if all *that* weren't enough, it's the name of the road in west London the group was named after!

B is for **blubbing.** Mel used to cry all the time when she was younger, getting really upset and frustrated because she hated shouting and losing her temper. Now she only cries when she gets really angry and reckons that being in the band has made her stronger. She says she hasn't cried for over a year.

C is for **condoms.** Mel confesses she never carries them around with her; she's not the kind of girl to act on impulse so she wouldn't need them. It appears that love lives and the music business are incompatible… Mel admits she's thinking of joining a nunnery!

D is for **dentist.** Crazy Nat Appleton reckons she would have liked to have gone to college and trained to be a dentist if she hadn't joined the group. She says she loved going to the dentist when she was younger and used to look forward to hearing the sound of the drill!

E is for **embarrassing excuses.** Nat's most embarrassing moment was when she was out on a date and a bird pooed on her head. She had to put on a baseball hat she happened to be carrying in her bag and made an excuse so that she could rush home!

F is for **flirting.** Nic prefers to flirt with people rather than chat them up! Shaznay describes Nic as the biggest flirt of them all and admits she'd have to be sure someone was flirting with her before she flirted back. Mel doesn't have Nic's confidence: she's shy and never flirts. In fact, Shaznay took up the

Nat's most embarrassing moment was when… a bird pooed on her head.

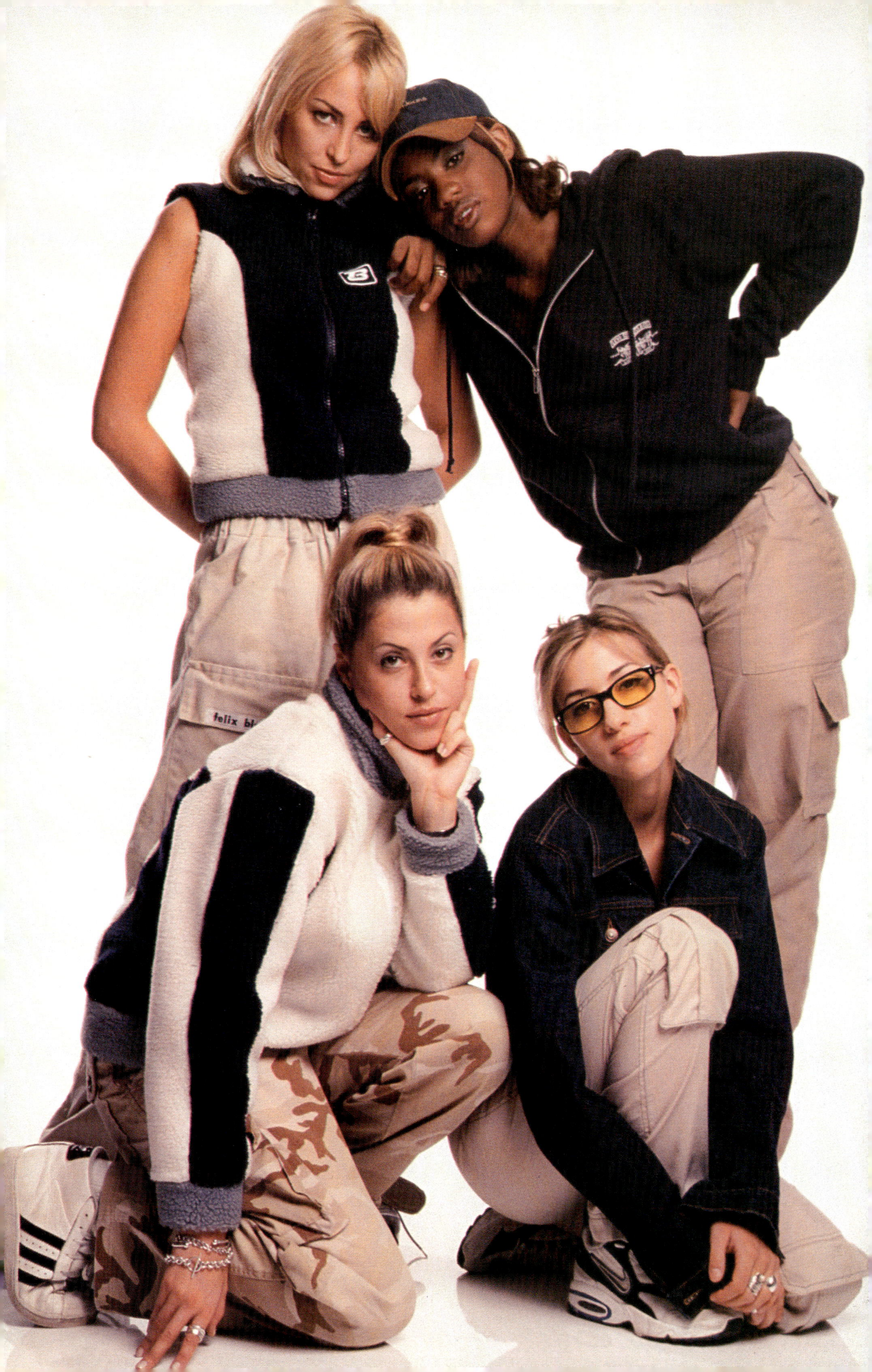

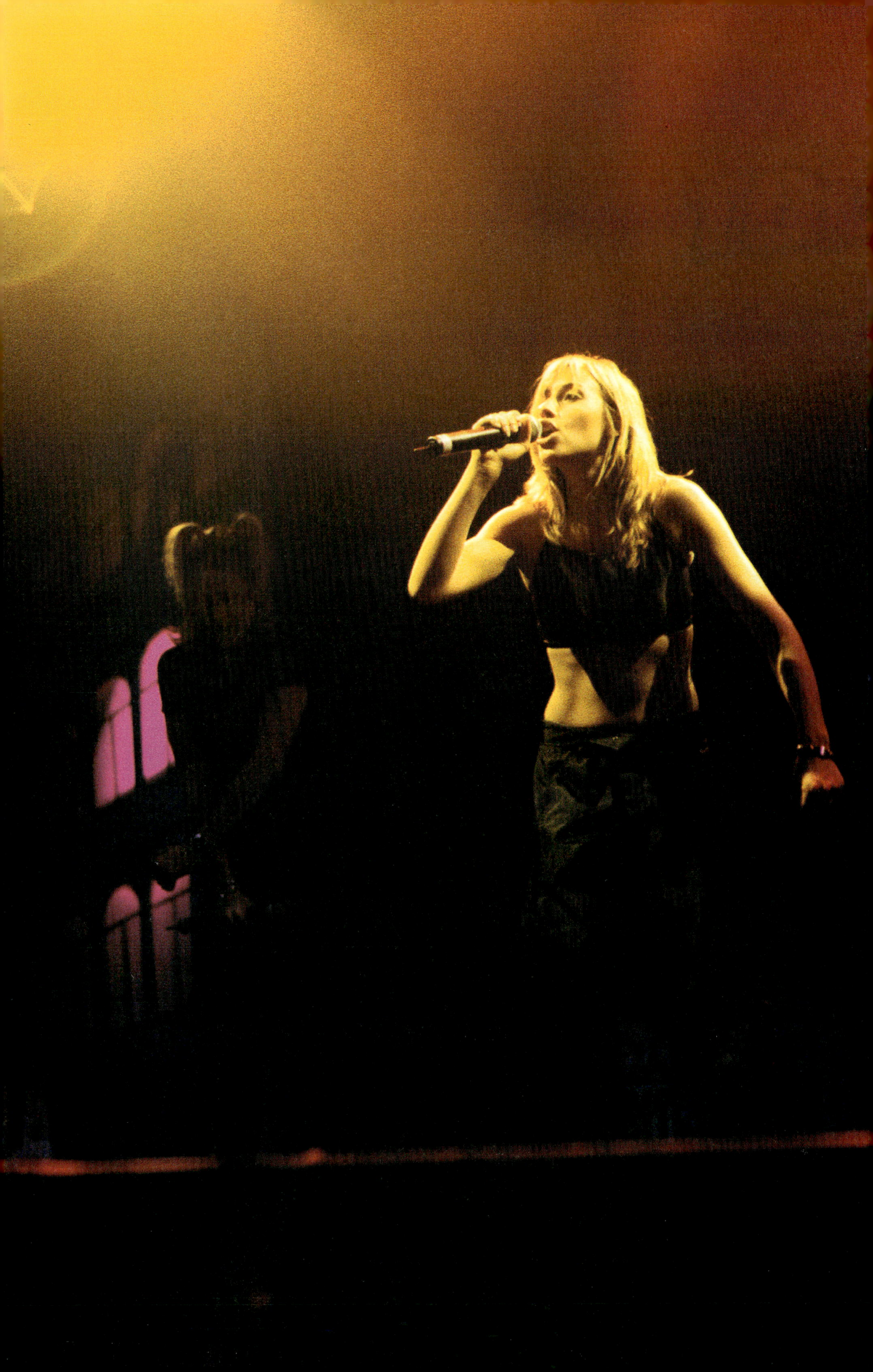

last offer Mel had because Ms Blatt just couldn't go through with it – she can't stand the thought of rejection!

G is for **Grange Hill.** When Nat had a small role in *Grange Hill* she dyed her hair especially for the occasion. Sadly, it went grey and looked absolutely *disgusting*!

H is for **heroine.** Shaznay once saved someone's life. She was walking down Oxford Street in London shopping when she came across a man lying in the road with blood pouring from his head. Everyone else was just stepping over him, but good ol' Shaz ran into the nearest shop for a bundle of tissues which she used to stop the bleeding until the ambulance arrived.

I is for **'I Know Where It's At',** the band's fantastic debut single released in August 1997. Written by Shaznay T. Lewis, its catchy swing-induced rhythm, rap segments and scratch effects were enough make your head spin. It reached Number 4 in the UK charts and kicked off the All Saints story.

J is for **junk food,** and, boy, do All Saints love it! Nat goes for pizzas, Chinese and McDonald's, while Shaznay also prefers burgers to posh nosh from trendy sandwich shops. If her friends were coming over she'd tell them to bring loads of popcorn, sweets and crisps. Nic reckons her ideal night in would be with a guy with loads of junk food in front of a scary film. Mel, on the other hand, is also a terrific cook… despite loving toasted peanut butter sandwiches!

K is for **kiss and tell.** Fame brings with it the unwanted attentions of the gutter press, looking for dirt to dish – but All Saints aren't worried about ex-boyfriends selling their stories. Mel says their ex-boyfriends are pretty decent guys and wouldn't do that. Shaznay agrees and thinks she's a very good judge of character… she's only had two boyfriends, anyway!

L is for **lies,** and when it comes to telling whoppers Nic's your gal! She says she used to lie compulsively at school and once told her schoolfriends that she kept seven pet wolves at home. She offered to let them see them in return for chocolate. She got loads of chocolate but never invited anyone home!

M is for **MOBO.** When All Saints performed at the Music Of Black Origin awards, Mel nearly wet herself with nerves! She was scared because all those peers she most respects were there and it was really important to her that they liked her music.

N is for **naked.** When they were asked to pose tastefully and naked on the cover of *Sky* magazine, the Saints turned it down. Mel says she thinks it's pathetic if you have to pose nude simply to get a cover of a magazine.

O is for **outrageous.** Shaznay had her nose pierced when she was at school, even though it wasn't allowed. She used to cover the ring with a plaster so teachers wouldn't see it!

Shaznay had her nose pierced when she was at school, even though it wasn't allowed.

P is for porn. Nat confesses the gals didn't watch rude films when they were young, but now they watch a lot of naughty pay-per-view movies on cable TV when they're away. Shaznay finds it 'a laugh'… and maybe it gives her ideas for lyrics!

Q is for quick buck. They're not in it to make fast money, says Mel – the music's the most important thing and they put their heart and soul into it. They like the money and the fancy clothes, though!

R is for R&B… or not! As Shaznay says, All Saints don't have a commercial R&B sound because Eternal do that – and they *don't* sound like Eternal. Nevertheless they take their influences from all sorts of music: hip-hop, pop, rock, dance… and R&B!

S is for… snogging. At last count, Nat reckons she's snogged more than 45 blokes!

T is for tabloids. Shaznay hates 'em, while Nat admits to being ever so slightly worried about what stories they cook up as she doesn't want to be embarrassed in front of her family.

U is for underwear. Nic has a theory that guys who can't dance also wear ugly underwear like Speedo pants in paisley! Oo-er!

V is for vocals. Natalie confesses she's scared of singing Shaz's vocals in front of her dad because of their content. That isn't surprising, since some of Shaznay's lyrics are raunchy to say the least!

W is for washing machine. Shaznay sucked her thumb all through her childhood, and when she was 16 her dentist told her she would have to wear a brace. Shaz said no because she was scared boys wouldn't want to snog her, but two years later she decided it *was* worth it, so she got one of those removable ones. Trouble is, Shaz kept losing it, often in the washing machine, so she eventually decided to have a permanent one.

X is for X-rated. Sultry songwriter Shaznay knows how to write steamy song words, and most of the album crackles with explicit lyrics. Is there something about Shaznay? According to her, she just looks at life the way it is. Hot stuff!

Y is for Yeeuurch! Mel admits that she has picked her nose and eaten it, but that she was 9 at the time and a whole group of her chums dared each other to do it. Enough said!

Z is for ZTT. All Saints, in their first incarnation, were briefly signed to ZTT Records – but, since neither group nor label knew what direction they wanted to go in, it was a pretty short-lived relationship.

A-Z of All Saints   **63**

Acknowledgements

Picture Credits

All Action
John Gladwin 6, 8, 28
John Mather 1, 7, 9 (bottom), 17, 22, 31, 42, 43, 51, 64

Big Pictures
30 (bottom), 62 (top)

Famous
Casper 2, 16, 19, 27, 32, 45, 46, 59, 61, 63
Walter Cornu 5 (left), 11, 12, 21, 24, 33, 34/35, 50, 56
F.Duval 44 (bottom)
Arjan Kleton 3, 52
Rudi Tucek 18, 54, 55

Pictorial Press
5 (right), 30 (top), 38, 58 (top), 60

Robert Lewis 13, 14, 15, 26, 29, 36, 39, 41, 47, 48, 49, 53, 58 (bottom)

Redferns
Kieran Doherty 37, 57, 62 (bottom)
Jill Douglas 10, 25, 40, 44 (top)
Michel Linssen 9 (top), 20, 23